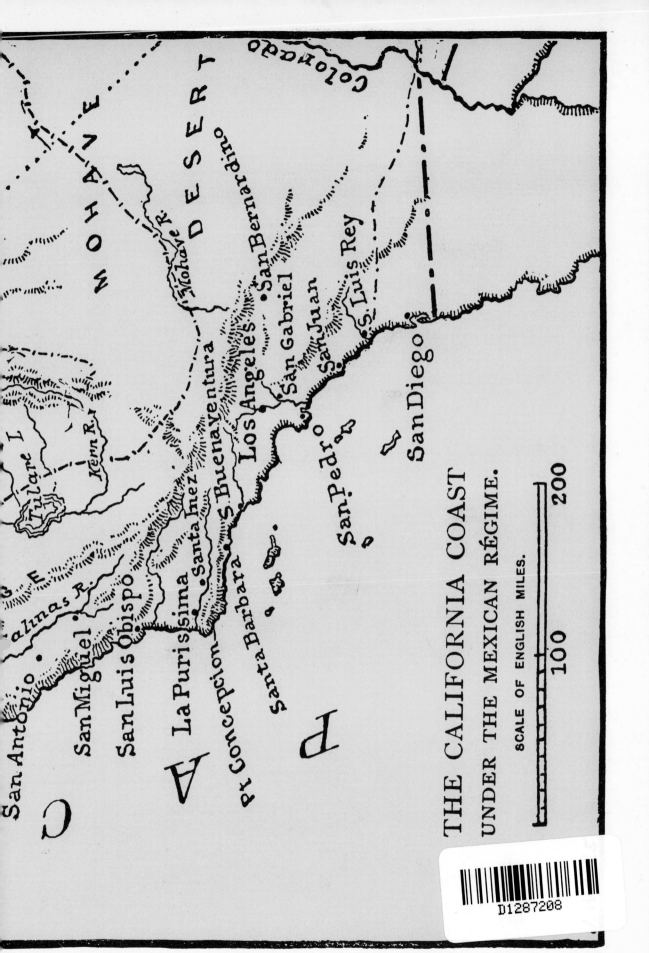

THE CALIFORNIA COAST
UNDER THE MEXICAN RÉGIME.

SCALE OF ENGLISH MILES.

100   200

THIS EDITION IS
LIMITED TO 1,950 COPIES.

LIFE IN CALIFORNIA
BEFORE THE
GOLD DISCOVERY

LIFE IN CALIFORNIA BEFORE THE GOLD DISCOVERY

BY
JOHN BIDWELL

—— ⚶ ——

FOREWORD
BY OSCAR LEWIS

LEWIS OSBORNE : PALO ALTO, 1966

FOREWORD

JOHN BIDWELL WAS BORN ON A FARM in western New York state on August 5, 1819. When he was twenty he left his parents' home in Ohio, spent some time on the Missouri-Iowa frontier, and in the spring of 1841 became a member of the first party of American settlers to set out for California. He arrived in the then-Mexican province in the fall of that year and a few weeks later joined the colony John A. Sutter had founded at the junction of the Sacramento and American rivers two years earlier. He continued to live there, and elsewhere in the Sacramento Valley, until his death in 1900. Thus he was a resident of California, and a close observer, during nearly six uncommonly eventful decades.

When, in the late 1880s, Bidwell wrote his reminiscenses of pioneer days in his adopted state, he had a wealth of experience from which to draw. He had witnessed—and more often than not played a significant part in—developments that had transformed the neglected and sparsely populated Mexican possession into one of the most populous states of the Union, and in the process made it the financial, industrial and agricultural center of the entire western third of the nation.

Almost from the beginning Bidwell played an important role in bringing that about. As Captain Sutter's trusted aide he supervised the dismantling of the Russian settlement at Fort Ross and the removal of its livestock and other property to his employer's headquarters in the valley. Later he managed Hock Farm, Sutter's ranch on the Feather River. Later still he took part in one of early California's bloodless revolutions, serving in the "army" Sutter had recruited to help Governor Micheltorena in his attempt to put down a revolt of dissatisfied Californians led by Juan Alvarado and José Castro.

After that campaign had ended in the defeat of the Micheltorena forces and the Governor's expulsion from the province, Bidwell returned to the Sacramento Valley and resumed his post as Sutter's right-hand man. Thus it happened that when, in the fall of 1846, John C. Frémont paid his second visit to California, he was in temporary charge at the fort during Sutter's absence. It was during Frémont's stay there that Bidwell gained his first —but not his last—knowledge of the imperious behavior of the temperamental Captain.

The next three years were the most eventful in California history, and Bidwell's presence at the fort during most of that period gave him an excellent vantage point for observation. Sutter's little settlement at New Helvetia was the only outpost of civilization in the entire central valley. Little of importance happened that was not to some degree influenced by events at and near the fort.

It was from there that, during the severe winter of 1846-47, four expeditions were sent to aid members of the Donner Party, trapped in the snows of the high Sierra. Frémont was a familiar figure at and about the fort during the months of his stay in California. The Bear Flag rebellion was planned by a group of Yankee settlers from the Sacramento Valley, and it was at the fort that Colonel Mariano G. Vallejo and two other Californians captured during the raid on Sonoma were held as prisoners. When, on the eve of the war with Mexico, Lieutenant Archibald Gillespie arrived bearing secret dispatches from Washington, Sutter provided him with a guide and other help that enabled him to overtake the departing Frémont party and bring about their return to the valley. Once active fighting broke out, Frémont established his headquarters at Sutter's Fort while he prepared his volunteer army for the invasion of the south. Finally, after the conquest of California had been completed— and only nine days before the signing of the Treaty of Guadalupe Hidalgo brought the war to a close—came a new sensation: the finding of gold at Sutter's Mill.

The rôle Bidwell played in the gold rush was unusual in one respect. To him, Marshall's discovery came as no great surprise, for—unlike the great majority of Californians—he had long believed that gold existed in the Sierra foothills. His first gold-seeking efforts were unsuccessful, but he continued the quest and eventually his persistence was rewarded. On July 4, 1848, while prospecting on the south fork of the Feather River, he located a claim so rich in gold that soon the entire district was swarming with miners. By 1853 the town that sprang up there —known as Bidwell's Bar—had a population of 2,000.

The profits from his mining operations permitted him to carry out a plan he had had in mind ever since he had left his Ohio home nearly ten years earlier: that of finding a tract of fertile farming land where he could settle down permanently. In 1849 he bought two properties in the upper Sacramento Valley, combined them into the Rancho Chico — which contained 26,000 acres — and there spent the remainder of his days.

Always an innovator, Bidwell was not long content to devote his ranch exclusively to raising cattle and sheep, as other land-owners in the valley were doing. He was one of the first to plant large acreage to wheat; soon, others followed his lead and during the next several decades the Sacramento and San Joaquin valleys produced a major share of the world's supply of that product.

By the early 1890s the wheat era was nearing its end, but long before that time Bidwell had begun putting his land to other uses. Orchards and vineyards were laid out and fields planted to berries, melons, and a variety of other crops. In order to deter-mine what types of fruit were best suited to the soil and climate of the valley he established what he called his experimental orchard; by the time of his death it covered 1,800 acres and con-tained upwards of 400 varieties of trees. In 1860 he laid out the town of Chico (present population about 18,500) on his prop-erty, setting aside ample space for parks, schools, churches, and other public uses. Two years later he began building his new home: an impressive, 22-room stone structure that stands in a grove of giant oak trees near the center of the town. There he lived until his death on April 4, 1900.

The memoirs reprinted here were first published in *The Century Magazine* for December, 1890 and February, 1891. Written late in life, long after the controversies and antagonisms of the period had subsided, their greatest value lies in the fact that they are the mature conclusions of one who wrote from first-hand knowledge.

In general, Bidwell's findings have stood the test of time. To be sure, later research has made clear that his memory was sometimes at fault—to cite one example, he was not, as he believed, the first to see the giant trees of the Sierra, the *Sequoia gigantea*. But such slips, as well as his occasional misspelling of proper names (Kearney for Kearny, Hudson Bay for Hudson's Bay) are minor defects in an account that provides present day readers with so detailed and engaging a picture of a bygone era.

—*Oscar Lewis*

P₄RT ONE

THE PARTY WHOSE FORTUNES I followed across the plains was not only the first that went direct to California from the East; we were probably the first white people, except Bonneville's party of 1833, that ever crossed the Sierra Nevada. Dr. Marsh's ranch, the first settlement reached by us in California, was located in the eastern foothills of the Coast Range Mountains, near the northwestern extremity of the great San Joaquin Valley and about six miles east of Monte Diablo, which may be called about the geographical center of Contra Costa County. There were no other settlements in the valley; it was, apparently, still just as new as when Columbus discovered America, and roaming over it were countless thousands of wild horses, of elk, and of antelope. It had been one of the driest years ever known in California. The country was brown and parched; throughout the State wheat, beans, everything had failed. Cattle were almost starving for grass, and the people, except perhaps a few of the best families, were without bread, and were eating chiefly meat, and that often of a very poor quality.

Dr. Marsh had come into California four or five years before by way of New Mexico. He was in some respects a remarkable man. In command of the English language I have scarcely ever seen his equal. He had never studied medicine, I believe, but was

16

a great reader: sometimes he would lie in bed all day reading, and he had a memory that stereotyped all he read, and in those days in California such a man could easily assume the role of doctor and practise medicine. In fact, with the exception of Dr. Marsh there was then no physician of any kind anywhere in California. We were overjoyed to find an American, and yet when we became acquainted with him we found him one of the most selfish of mortals. The night of our arrival he killed two pigs for us. We felt very grateful, for we had by no means recovered from starving on poor mule meat, and when he set his Indian cook to making tortillas (little cakes) for us, giving one to each,—there were thirty-two in our party,—we felt even more grateful; and especially when we learned that he had had to use some of his seed wheat, for he had no other. Hearing that there was no such thing as money in the country, and that butcher-knives, guns, ammunition, and everything of that kind were better than money, we expressed our gratitude the first night to the doctor by presents —one giving a can of powder, another a bar of lead or a butcher-knife, and another a cheap but serviceable set of surgical instruments. The next morning I rose early, among the first, in order to learn from our host something about California,—what we could do, and where we could go,—and, strange as it may seem, he would scarcely answer a question. He seemed to be in an ill humor, and among other things he said, "The company has already been over a hundred dollars' expense to me, and God knows whether I will ever get a *real* of it or not." I was at a loss to account for this, and went out and told some of the party, and found that others had been snubbed in a similar manner. We held a consultation and resolved to leave as soon as convenient.

TULE MARSH IN THE SAN JOACHIN RIVER VALLEY.

Half our party concluded to go back to the San Joaquin River, where there was much game, and spend the winter hunting, chiefly for otter, the skins being worth three dollars apiece. The rest—about fourteen—succeeded in gaining information from Dr. Marsh by which they started to find the town of San José, about forty miles to the south, then known by the name of Pueblo de San José, now the city of San José. More or less of our effects had to be left at Marsh's, and I decided to remain and look out for them, and meantime to make short excursions about the country on my own account. After the others had left I started off traveling south, and came to what is now called Livermore Valley, then known as Livermore's Ranch, belonging to

Robert Livermore, a native of England. He had left a vessel when a mere boy, and had married and lived like the native Californians, and, like them, was very expert with the lasso. Livermore's was the frontier ranch, and more exposed than any other to the ravages of the Horse-thief Indians of the Sierra Nevada. That valley was full of wild cattle,—thousands of them,—and they were more dangerous to one on foot, as I was, than grizzly bears. By dodging into the gulches and behind trees I made my way to a Mexican ranch at the extreme west end of the valley, where I staid all night. This was one of the noted ranches, and belonged to a Californian called Don José Maria Amador—more recently, to a man named Dougherty.[1] Next day, seeing nothing to encourage me, I started to return to Marsh's ranch.

On the way, as I came to where two roads, or rather paths, converged, I fell in with one of the fourteen men, M. C. Nye, who had started for San José. He seemed considerably agitated, and reported that at the Mission of San José, some fifteen miles this side of the town of San José, all the men had been arrested and put in prison by General Vallejo, Mexican commander-in-chief of the military under Governor Alvarado, he alone having been sent back to tell Marsh and have him come forthwith to

---

[1] The rancheros marked and branded their stock differently so as to distinguish them. But it was not possible to keep them separate. One would often steal cattle from the other. Livermore in this way lost cattle by his neighbor Amador. In fact it was almost a daily occurrence — a race to see which could get and kill the most of the other's cattle. Cattle in those days were often killed for the hides alone. One day a man saw Amador kill a fine steer belonging to Livermore. When he reached Livermore's — ten or fifteen miles away — and told him what Amador had done, he found Livermore skinning a steer of Amador's!

MISSION SAN JOSÉ.

explain why this armed force had invaded the country. We reached Marsh's after dark. The next day the doctor started down to the Mission of San José, nearly thirty miles distant, with a list of the company, which I gave him. He was gone about three days. Meanwhile we sent word to the men on the San Joaquin River to let them know what had taken place, and they at once returned to the ranch to await results. When Marsh came back he said ominously, "Now, men, I want you all to come into the house and I will tell you your fate." We all went in and he announced, "You men that have five dollars can have passports and remain in the country and go where you please." The fact was he had simply obtained passports for the asking; they had cost him nothing. The men who had been arrested at the Mission had been liberated as soon as their passports were issued to them, and they had at once proceeded on their way to San José. But five dollars! I don't suppose any one had five dollars; nine-tenths of them probably had not a cent of money. The names were called and each man settled, giving the amount in something, and if unable to make it up in money or effects he would give his note for the rest. All the names were called except my own. There was no passport for me. Marsh had certainly not forgotten me, for I had furnished him with the list of our names myself. Possibly his idea was—as others surmised and afterwards told me—that, lacking a passport, I would stay at his ranch and make a useful hand to work.

The next morning before day found me starting for the Mission of San José to get a passport for myself. Mike Nye, the man who had brought the news of the arrest, went with me. A friend had lent me a poor old horse, fit only to carry my blankets. I arrived in a heavy rain-storm, and was marched into the calaboose and kept there three days with nothing to eat, and the fleas were so numerous as to cover and darken anything of a light color. There were four or five Indians in the prison. They were ironed, and they kept tolling a bell as a punishment, I suppose, for they were said to have stolen horses; possibly they belonged to the Horse-thief tribes east of the San Joaquin Valley. Sentries were stationed at the door. Through a grated window I made a motion to an Indian boy outside and he brought me a handful of beans and a handful of *manteca*, which is used by Mexicans instead of lard. It seemed as if they were going to starve me to death. After having been there three days I saw through the door a man whom, from his light hair, I took to be an American, although he was clad in the wild picturesque garb of a native Californian, including serape and the huge spurs used by the vaquero. I had the sentry at the door hail him. He proved to be an American, a resident of the Pueblo of San José, named Thomas Bowen, and he kindly went to Vallejo, who was right across the way in the big Mission building, and procured for me the passport. I think I have that passport now, signed by Vallejo and written in Spanish by Victor Prudon, secretary of Vallejo. Every one at the Mission pronounced Marsh's action an outrage; such a thing was never known before.

We had already heard that a man by the name of Sutter was starting a colony a hundred miles away to the north in the Sacramento Valley. No other civilized settlements had been attempted anywhere east of the Coast Range; before Sutter came the Indians had reigned supreme. As the best thing to be done I now determined to go to Sutter's, afterward called "Sutter's Fort," or New Helvetia. Dr. Marsh said we could make the journey in two days, but it took us eight. Winter had come in earnest, and winter in California then, as now, meant rain. I had three companions. It was wet when we started, and much of the time we traveled through a pouring rain. Streams were out of their banks; gulches were swimming; plains were inundated; indeed, most of the country was overflowed. There were no roads, merely paths, trodden only by Indians and wild game. We were compelled to follow the paths, even when they were under water, for the moment our animals stepped to one side down they went into the mire. Most of the way was through the region now lying between Lathrop and Sacramento. We got out of provisions and were about three days without food. Game was plentiful, but hard to shoot in the rain. Besides, it was impossible to keep our old flint-lock guns dry, and especially the powder dry in the pans. On the eighth day we came to Sutter's settlement; the fort had not then been begun. Sutter received us with open arms and in a princely fashion, for he was a man of the most polite address and the most courteous manners, a man who could shine in any society. Moreover, our coming was not unexpected to him. It will be remembered that in the Sierra Nevada one of our men named Jimmy John became separated from the main party. It seems that he came on into California, and, diverging into the north, found his way down to Sutter's settlement perhaps a little before we reached Dr. Marsh's. Through this man Sutter heard that our company of thirty men were already somewhere in California. He immediately loaded two mules with provisions taken out of his private stores, and sent two men with them in search of us. But they did not find us, and returned, with the provisions, to Sutter's. Later, after a long search, the same two men, having been sent out again by Sutter, struck our trail and followed it to Marsh's.

John A. Sutter was born in Baden in 1803 of Swiss parents, and was proud of his connection with the only republic of consequence in Europe. He was a warm admirer of the United States, and some of his friends had persuaded him to come across the Atlantic. He first went to a friend in Indiana with whom he staid awhile, helping to clear land, but it was business that he was not accustomed to. So he made his way to St. Louis and invested what means he had in merchandise, and went out as a New Mexican trader to Santa Fé. Having been unsuccessful at Santa Fé, he returned to St. Louis, joined a party of trappers, went to the Rocky Mountains, and found his way down the Columbia River to Fort Vancouver. There he formed plans for trying to get down to the coast of California to establish a colony. He took a vessel that went to the Sandwich Islands, and there communicated his plans to people who assisted him. But as there was no vessel going direct from the Sandwich Islands to Cali-

JOHN A. SUTTER
(FROM A PHOTOGRAPH BY BRADLEY & RULOFSON)

fornia, he had to take a Russian vessel by way of Sitka. He got such credit and help as he could in the Sandwich Islands and induced five or six natives to accompany him to start the contemplated colony. He expected to send to Europe and the United States for his colonists. When he came to the coast of California, in 1840, he had an interview with the governor, Alvarado, and obtained permission to explore the country and find a place for his colony. He came to the bay of San Francisco, procured a small boat and explored the largest river he could find, and selected the site where the city of Sacramento now stands.

A short time before we arrived Sutter had bought out the Russian-American Fur Company at Fort Ross and Bodega on the Pacific. That company had a charter from Spain to take furs, but

Old Fort Ross.

had no right to the land. The charter had about expired. Against the protest of the California authorities they had extended their settlement southward some twenty miles farther than they had any right to, and had occupied the country to, and even beyond, the bay of Bodega. The time came when the taking of furs was no longer profitable; the Russians were ordered to vacate and return to Sitka. They wished to sell out all their personal property and whatever remaining right they had to the land. So Sutter bought them out — cattle and horses; a little vessel of about twenty-five tons burden, called a launch; and other property, including forty odd pieces of old rusty cannon and one or two small brass pieces, with a quantity of old French flint-lock muskets pronounced by Sutter to be of those lost by Bonaparte in 1812 in his disastrous retreat from Moscow. This ordnance Sutter conveyed up the Sacramento River on the launch to his colony. As soon as the native Californians heard that he had bought out the Russians and was beginning to fortify himself by taking up the cannon they began to fear him. They were doubtless jealous because Americans and other foreigners had already commenced to make the place their headquarters, and they foresaw that Sutter's fort would be for them, especially for Americans, what it naturally did become in fact, a place of protection and general rendezvous; and so they threatened to break it up. Sutter had not as yet actually received his grant; he had simply taken preliminary steps and had obtained permission to settle and proceed to colonize. These threats were made before he had begun the fort, much less built it, and Sutter felt insecure. He had a good many Indians whom he had collected about him, and a few white men (perhaps fifteen or twenty) and some Sandwich Islanders.

When he heard of the coming of our thirty men he inferred at once that we would soon reach him and be an additional protection. With this feeling of security, even before the arrival of our party Sutter was so indiscreet as to write a letter to the governor or to some one in authority, saying that he wanted to hear no more threats of dispossession, for he was now able not only to defend himself but to go and chastise them. That letter having been despatched to the city of Mexico, the authorities there sent a new governor in 1842 with about six hundred troops to subdue Sutter. But the new governor, Manuel Micheltorena, was an intelligent man. He knew the history of California and was aware that nearly all of his predecessors had been expelled by insurrections of the native Californians. Sutter sent a courier to meet the governor before his arrival at Los Angeles, with a letter in French, conveying his greetings to the governor, expressing a most cordial welcome, and submitting cheerfully and entirely to his authority. In this way the governor and Sutter became fast friends, and through Sutter the Americans had a friend in Governor Micheltorena.

The first employment I had in California was in Sutter's service, about two months after our arrival at Marsh's. He engaged me to go to Bodega and Fort Ross and to stay there until he could finish removing the property which he had bought from the Russians. I remained there fourteen months, until everything was removed; then I came up into Sacramento Valley and took charge for Sutter of his Hock farm (so named from a large Indian village on the place), remaining there a little more than a year— in 1843 and part of 1844.

Nearly everybody who came to California made it a point to

reach Sutter's Fort.[1] Sutter was one of the most liberal and hospitable of men. Everybody was welcome—one man or a hundred, it was all the same. He had peculiar traits: his necessities compelled him to take all he could buy, and he paid all he could pay; but he failed to keep up with his payments. And so he soon found himself immensely — almost hopelessly — involved in debt. His debt to the Russians amounted at first to something near one hundred thousand dollars. Interest increased apace. He had agreed to pay in wheat, but his crops failed. He struggled in every way, sowing large areas to wheat, increasing his cattle and horses, and trying to build a flouring mill. He kept his launch running to and from the bay, carrying down hides, tallow, furs, wheat, etc., returning with lumber sawed by hand in the redwood groves nearest the bay and other supplies. On an average it took a month to make a trip. The fare for each person was five dollars, including board. Sutter started many other new enterprises in order to find relief from his embarrassments; but, in

---

[1] Every year after the arrival of our party, in 1841, immigrant parties came across the plains to California; except in 1842, when they went to Oregon, most of them coming thence to California in 1843. Ours of 1841 being the first, let me add that a later party arrived in California in 1841. It was composed of about twenty-five persons who arrived at Westport, Mo., too late to come with us, and so went with the annual caravan of St. Louis traders to Santa Fé, and thence *via* the Gila River into Southern California.

Among the more noted arrivals on this coast I may mention:

1841.—Commodore Wilkes's Exploring Expedition, a party of which came overland from Oregon to California, under Captain Ringgold, I think.

1842.—Commodore Thomas ap Catesby Jones, who raised the American flag in Monterey.

1843.—*First.* L. W. Hastings, *via* Oregon. He was ambitious to make California a republic and to be its first president, and wrote an iridescent

spite of all he could do, these increased. Every year found him worse and worse off; but it was partly his own fault. He employed men—not because he always needed and could profitably employ them, but because in the kindness of his heart it simply became a habit to employ everybody who wanted employment. As long as he had anything he trusted any one with everything he wanted —responsible or otherwise, acquaintances and strangers alike. Most of the labor was done by Indians, chiefly wild ones, except a few from the Missions who spoke Spanish. The wild ones learned Spanish so far as they learned anything, that being the language of the country, and everybody had to learn something of it. The number of men employed by Sutter may be stated at from 100 to 500—the latter number at harvest time. Among them were blacksmiths, carpenters, tanners, gunsmiths, vaqueros, farmers, gardeners, weavers (to weave coarse woolen blankets), hunters, sawyers (to saw lumber by hand, a custom known in England), sheep-herders, trappers, and, later, millwrights and a distiller. In a word, Sutter started every business and enterprise

---

book to induce immigration,—which came in 1846,—but found the American flag flying when he returned with the immigration he had gone to meet. Also among the noted arrivals in 1843 was Pierson B. Reading, an accomplished gentleman, the proprietor of Reading's ranch in Shasta County, and from whom Fort Reading took its name. Samuel J. Hensley was also one of the same party. *Second.* Dr. Sandels, a very intelligent man.

1844.—*First.* Frémont's first arrival (in March); Mr. Charles Preuss, a scientific man, and Kit Carson with him. *Second.* The Stevens-Townsend-Murphy party, who brought the first wagons into California across the plains.

1845.—*First.* James W. Marshall, who, in 1848, discovered the gold. *Second.* Frémont's second arrival, also Hastings's second arrival.

1846.—Largest immigration party, the one Hastings went to meet. The Donner party was among the last of these immigrants.

SUTTER'S FORT.

possible. He tried to maintain a sort of military discipline. Cannon were mounted, and pointed in every direction through embrasures in the walls and bastions. The soldiers were Indians, and every evening after coming from work they were drilled under a white officer, generally a German, marching to the music of fife and drum. A sentry was always at the gate, and regular bells called men to and from work.

Harvesting, with the rude implements, was a scene. Imagine three or four hundred wild Indians in a grain field, armed, some with sickles, some with butcher-knives, some with pieces of hoop iron roughly fashioned into shapes like sickles, but many having only their hands with which to gather by small handfuls the dry and brittle grain; and as their hands would soon become sore, they resorted to dry willow sticks, which were split to afford a

30

sharper edge with which to sever the straw. But the wildest part was the threshing. The harvest of weeks, sometimes of a month, was piled up in the straw in the form of a huge mound in the middle of a high, strong, round corral; then three or four hundred wild horses were turned in to thresh it, the Indians whooping to make them run faster. Suddenly they would dash in before the band at full speed, when the motion became reversed, with the effect of plowing up the trampled straw to the very bottom. In an hour the grain would be thoroughly threshed and the dry straw broken almost into chaff. In this manner I have seen two thousand bushels of wheat threshed in a single hour. Next came the winnowing, which would often take another month. It could only be done when the wind was blowing, by throwing high into the air shovelfuls of grain, straw, and chaff, the lighter materials being wafted to one side, while the grain, comparatively clean, would descend and form a heap by itself. In this manner all the grain in California was cleaned. At that day no such thing as a fanning mill had ever been brought to this coast.

The kindness and hospitality of the native Californians have not been overstated. Up to the time the Mexican régime ceased in California they had a custom of never charging for anything; that is to say, for entertainment—food, use of horses, etc. You were supposed, even if invited to visit a friend, to bring your blankets with you, and one would be very thoughtless if he traveled and did not take a knife with him to cut his meat. When you had eaten, the invariable custom was to rise, deliver to the woman or hostess the plate on which you had eaten the meat and beans—for that was about all they had—and say, *"Muchas gracias, Señora"* ("Many thanks, madame"); and the hostess as

A bit of the Coast Range.

invariably replied, *"Buen provecho"* ("May it do you much good"). The Missions in California invariably had gardens with grapes, olives, figs, pomegranates, pears, and apples, but the ranches scarcely ever had any fruit. When you wanted a horse to ride, you would take it to the next ranch—it might be twenty, thirty, or fifty miles—and turn it out there, and sometime or other in reclaiming his stock the owner would get it back. In this way you might travel from one end of California to the other.

The ranch life was not confined to the country, it prevailed in the towns too. There was not a hotel in San Francisco, or Monterey, or anywhere in California, till 1846, when the Americans took the country. The priests at the Missions were glad to entertain strangers without charge. They would give you a room in which to sleep, and perhaps a bedstead with a hide stretched across it, and over that you would spread your blankets.

At this time there was not in California any vehicle except a rude California cart; the wheels were without tires, and were made by felling an oak tree and hewing it down till it made a solid wheel nearly a foot thick on the rim and a little larger where the axle went through. The hole for the axle would be eight or nine inches in diameter, but a few years' use would increase it to a foot. To make the hole, an auger, gouge, or chisel was sometimes used, but the principal tool was an ax. A small tree required but little hewing and shaping to answer for an axle. These carts were always drawn by oxen, the yoke being lashed with rawhide to the horns. To lubricate the axles they used soap (that is one thing the Mexicans could make), carrying along for the purpose a big pail of thick soapsuds which was constantly put in the box or hole; but you could generally tell when a Cali-

A California cart.

THE GOVERNOR'S EQUIPAGE.

fornia cart was coming half a mile away by the squeaking. I have seen the families of the wealthiest people go long distances at the rate of thirty miles or more a day, visiting in one of these clumsy two-wheeled vehicles. They had a little framework around it made of round sticks, and a bullock hide was put in for a floor or bottom. Sometimes the better class would have a little calico for curtains and cover. There was no such thing as a spoked wheel in use then. Somebody sent from Boston a wagon as a present to the priest in charge of the Mission of San José, but as soon as summer came the woodwork shrunk, the tires came off, and it all fell to pieces. There was no one in California to set tires. When Governor Micheltorena was sent from Mexico to California he brought with him an ambulance, not much better than a common spring wagon, such as a marketman would now use with one horse. It had shafts, but in California at that time there was no horse broken to work in them, nor was there such a thing known as a harness; so the governor had two mounted vaqueros to pull it, their reatas being fastened to the shafts and to the pommels of their saddles. The first wagons brought into California came across the plains in 1844 with the Townsend or Stevens party. They were left in the mountains and lay buried under the snow till the following spring, when Moses Schallenberger, Elisha Stevens (who was the captain of the party), and others went up and brought some of the wagons down into the Sacramento Valley. No other wagons had ever before reached California across the plains.

Elisha Stevens was from Georgia and had there worked in the gold mines. He started across the plains with the express purpose of finding gold. When he got into the Rocky Mountains, as I was told by his friend Dr. Townsend, Stevens said, "We are in a gold country." One evening (when they camped for the night) he went into a gulch, took some gravel and washed it and got the color of gold, thus unmistakably showing, as he afterwards did in Lower California, that he had considerable knowledge of gold mining. But the strange thing is, that afterwards, when he passed up and down several times over the country between Bear and Yuba rivers, as he did with the party in the spring of 1845 to bring down their wagons, he should have seen no signs of gold where subsequently the whole country was found to contain it.

The early foreign residents of California were largely runaway sailors. Many if not most would change their names. For instance, Gilroy's ranch, where the town of Gilroy is now located, was owned by an old resident under the assumed appellation of Gilroy. Of course vessels touching upon this coast were liable, as they were everywhere, to lose men by desertion, especially if

A RUNAWAY SAILOR.

the men were maltreated. Such things have been so common that it is not difficult to believe that those who left their vessels in early days on this then distant coast had cause for so doing. To be known as a runaway sailor was no stain upon a man's character. It was no uncommon thing, after my arrival here, for sailors to be skulking and hiding about from ranch to ranch till the vessel they had left should leave the coast. At Amador's ranch, before mentioned, on my first arrival here, I met a sailor boy, named Harrison Pierce, of eighteen or twenty years, who was concealing himself till his vessel should go to sea. He managed to escape recapture and so remained in the country. He was one of the men who went with me from Marsh's ranch to Sutter's. Californians would catch and return sailors to get the reward which, I believe, captains of vessels invariably offered. After the vessels had sailed and there was no chance of the reward, the native Californians gave the fugitives no further trouble.

At that time the only trade, foreign or domestic, was in hides, tallow, and furs; but mostly hides. With few exceptions the vessels that visited the coast were from Boston, fitted out by Hooper to go there and trade for hides. Occasionally vessels would put in for water or in distress. San Francisco was the principal harbor; the next was Monterey. There was an anchorage off San Luis Obispo; the next was Santa Barbara, the next San Buenaventura, then San Pedro, and lastly San Diego. The hides were generally collected and brought to San Diego and there salted, staked out to dry, and folded so that they would lie compactly in the ship, and thence were shipped to Boston. Goods were principally sold on board the vessels: there were very few stores on land; that of Thomas O. Larkin at Monterey was the principal one. The entrance of a vessel into harbor or roadstead was a signal to all the ranchers to come in their little boats and launches laden with hides to trade for goods. Thus vessels went from port to port, remaining few or many days according to the amount of trade. When the people stopped bringing hides, a vessel would leave.

I have said that there was no regular physician in California. Later, in 1843, in a company that came from Oregon, was one Joe Meeks, a noted character in the Rocky Mountains. On the way he said, "Boys, when I get down to California among the Greasers I am going to palm myself off as a doctor"; and from that time they dubbed him Dr. Meeks. He could neither read nor write. As soon as the Californians heard of his arrival at Monterey they began to come to him with their different ailments.

His first professional service was to a boy who had a toe cut off. Meeks, happening to be near, stuck the toe on, binding it in a poultice of mud, and it grew on again. The new governor, Micheltorena, employed him as surgeon. Meeks had a way of looking and acting very wise, and of being reticent when people talked about things which he did not understand. One day he went into a little shop kept by a man known as Dr. Stokes, who had been a kind of hospital steward on board ship, and who had brought ashore one of those little medicine chests that were usually taken to sea, with apothecary scales, and a pamphlet giving a short synopsis of diseases and a table of weights and medicines, so that almost anybody could administer relief to sick sailors. Meeks went to him and said, "Doctor, I want you to put me up some powders." So Stokes went behind his table and got out his scales and medicines, and asked, "What kind of powders?" "Just common powders—patient not very sick." "If you will tell me what kind of powders, Dr. Meek—" "Oh, just common powders." That is all he would say. Dr. Stokes told about town that Meeks knew nothing about medicine, but people thought that perhaps Meeks had given the prescription in Latin and that Dr. Stokes could not read it. But Meeks's reign was to have an end. An American man-of-war came into the harbor. Thomas O. Larkin was then the United States consul at Monterey, and the commander and all his officers went up to Larkin's store, among them the surgeon, who was introduced to Dr. Meeks. The conversation turning upon the diseases incident to the country, Meeks became reticent, saying merely that he was going out of practice and intended to leave the country, because he could not get medicines. The surgeon expressed much sympathy and said, "Dr. Meeks, if you will make me out a list I will very cheerfully divide with you such medicines as I can spare." Meeks did not know the names of three kinds of medicine, and tried evasion, but the surgeon cornered him and put the question so direct that he had to answer. He asked him what medicine he needed most. Finally Meeks said he wanted some "draps," and that was all that could be got out of him. When the story came out his career as a doctor was at an end, and he soon after left the country.

In 1841 there was likewise no lawyer in California. In 1843 a lawyer named Hastings arrived *via* Oregon. He was an ambitious man, and desired to wrest the country from Mexico and make it a republic. He disclosed his plan to a man who revealed it to me. His scheme was to go down to Mexico and make friends of the Mexican authorities, if possible get a grant of land, and then go into Texas, consult President Houston, and go East and write a book, praising the country to the skies, which he did, with little regard to accuracy. His object was to start a large immigration, and in this he succeeded. The book was published in 1845, and undoubtedly largely induced what was called the "great immigration" of 1846 across the plains, consisting of about six hundred. Hastings returned to California in the autumn of 1845, preparatory to taking steps to declare the country independent and to establish a republic and make himself president. In 1846 he went back to meet the immigration and to perfect his plans so that the emigrants would know exactly where to go and what to do. But in 1846 the Mexican war intervened, and while Hastings was gone to meet the immigration California was taken possession of by the United States. These doubtless were the first plans ever conceived for the independence of California.

38

TWO ARRIVALS FROM ACROSS THE PLAINS.

Hastings knew there were not enough Americans and foreigners yet in California to do anything. He labored hard to get money to publish his book, and went about lecturing on temperance in Ohio, where he became intimate with a fellow by the name of McDonald, who was acting the Methodist preacher and pretending, with considerable success, to raise funds for missionary purposes. At last they separated, McDonald preceding Hastings to San Francisco, where he became bartender for a man named Vioget, who owned a saloon and a billiard table — the first, I think, on the Pacific coast. Hastings returned later, and, reaching San Francisco in a cold rain, went up to Vioget's and called for brandy. He poured out a glassful and was about to drink it, when McDonald, recognizing him, leaned over the bar, extended his hand, and said, "My good temperance friend, how are you?" Hastings in great surprise looked him in the eyes, recognized him, and said, "My dear Methodist brother, how do you do?"

It is not generally known that in 1841 — the year I reached California — gold was discovered in what is now a part of Los Angeles County. The yield was not rich; indeed, it was so small that it made no stir. The discoverer was an old Canadian Frenchman by the name of Baptiste Ruelle, who had been a trapper with the Hudson Bay Company, and, as was not an infrequent case with those trappers, had drifted down into New Mexico, where he had worked in placer mines. The mines discovered by Ruelle in California attracted a few New Mexicans, by whom they were worked for several years. But as they proved too poor, Ruelle himself came up into the Sacramento Valley, five hundred miles away, and engaged to work for Sutter when I was in Sutter's service.[1] Now it so happened that almost every year a party of a dozen men or more would come from or return to Oregon. Of such parties some—perhaps most of them—would be Canadian French, who had trapped all over the country, and these were generally the guides. In 1843 it was known to every one that such a party was getting ready to go to Oregon. Baptiste Ruelle had been in Sutter's employ several months, when one day he came to Sutter, showed him a few small particles of gold, and said he had found them on the American River, and he wanted to go far into the mountains on that stream to prospect for gold. For this purpose he desired two mules loaded with provisions, and he selected two notedly stupid Indian boys whom he wanted to go into the mountains with him, saying he would have no others. Of course, he did not get the outfit. Sutter and I talked about it and queried, What does he want with so much provision — the American River being only a mile and the mountains only twenty miles distant? And why does he want those two stupid boys, since he might be attacked by the Indians? Our conclusion was that he really wanted the outfit so that he could join the party and go to Oregon and remain. Such I believe was Ruelle's intention; though in 1848, after James W. Marshall had discovered the gold at Coloma, Ruelle, who was one of the first to go there and mine, still protested that he had discovered gold on the American River in 1843. The only thing that I can recall to lend the least plausibility to Ruelle's pretensions would be that, so

---

[1] New Mexican miners invariably carried their gold (which was generally small, and small in quantity as well) in a large quill—that of a vulture or turkey buzzard. Sometimes these quills would hold three or four ounces, and, being translucent, they were graduated so as to see at any time the quantity in them. The gold was kept in by a stopper. Ruelle had such a quill, which appeared to have been carried for years.

far as I know, he never, after that one time, manifested any desire to go to Oregon, and remained in California till he died. But I should add, neither did he ever show any longing again to go into the mountains to look for gold during the subsequent years he remained with Sutter, even to the time of Marshall's discovery.

Early in the spring of 1844, a Mexican working under me at the Hock Farm for Sutter came to me and told me there was gold in the Sierra Nevada. His name was Pablo Gutierrez. The discovery by Marshall, it will be remembered, was in January, 1848. Pablo told me this at a time when I was calling him to account because he had absented himself the day before without permission. I was giving him a lecture in Spanish, which I could speak quite well in those days. Like many Mexicans, he had an Indian wife; some time before, he had been in the mountains and had bought a squaw. She had run away from him, and he had gone to find and bring her back. And it was while he was on this trip, he said, that he had seen signs of gold. After my lecture he said, "Señor, I have made an important discovery; there surely is gold on Bear River in the mountains." This was in March, 1844. A few days afterward I arranged to go with him up on Bear River. We went five or six miles into the mountains, when he showed me the signs and the place where he thought the gold was. "Well," I said, "can you not find some?" No, he said, because he must have a *batea*. He talked so much about the "batea" that I concluded it must be a complicated machine. "Can't Mr. Keiser, our saddle-tree maker, make the batea?" I asked. "Oh, no." I did not then know that a batea is nothing more nor less than a wooden bowl which the Mexicans use for washing gold. I said, "Pablo, where can you get it?" He said, "Down in Mexico." I said, "I will help pay your expenses if you will go down and get one," which he promised to do. I said, "Pablo, say nothing to anybody else about this gold discovery, and we will get the batea and find the gold." As time passed I was afraid to let him go to Mexico, lest when he got among his relatives he might be induced to stay and not come back, so I made a suggestion to him. I said, "Pablo, let us save our earnings and get on a vessel and go around to Boston, and there get the batea; I can interpret for you, and the Yankees are very ingenious and can make anything." The idea pleased him, and he promised to go as soon as we could save enough to pay our expenses. He was to keep it a secret, and I believe he faithfully kept his promise. It would have taken us a year or two to get money enough to go. In those days there were every year four or five arrivals, sometimes six, of vessels laden with goods from Boston to trade for hides in California. These vessels brought around all classes of goods needed by the Mexican people. It would have required about six months each way, five months being a quick passage. But, as will be seen, our plans were interrupted. In the autumn of that year, 1844, a revolt took place. The native chiefs of California, José Castro and ex-Governor Alvarado, succeeded in raising an insurrection against the Mexican governor, Micheltorena, to expel him from the country. They accused him of being friendly to Americans and of giving them too much land. The truth was, he had simply shown impartiality. When Americans had been here long enough, had conducted themselves properly, and had complied with the colonization laws of Mexico, he had given them lands as readily as to native-born citizens. He was a fair-minded man and an intelligent and good governor, and wished to develop the country. His friendship for Americans was a mere pretext; for his first predecessor, Alvarado, and his successors, Pio Pico, also granted lands freely to foreigners, and among them to Americans. The real cause of the insurrection against Micheltorena, however, was that the native chiefs had become hungry to get hold again of the revenues. The feeling against Americans was easily aroused and became their main excuse. The English and French influence, so far as felt, evidently leaned towards the side of the Californians. It was not open but it was felt, and not a few expressed the hope that England or France would some day seize and hold California. I believe the Gachupines—natives of Spain, of whom there were a few—did not participate in the feeling against the Americans, though few did much, if anything, to allay it. In October Sutter went from Sacramento to Monterey, the capital, to see the governor. I went with him. On our way thither, at San José, we heard the first mutterings of the insurrection. We hastened to Monterey, and were the first to communicate the fact to the governor. Sutter, alarmed, took the first opportunity to get away by water. There were in those days no mail routes, no public conveyances of any kind, no regular line of travel, no public highways. But a vessel happened to touch at Monterey, and Sutter took passage to the bay of San Francisco, and thence by his own launch reached home. In a few days the first blow was struck, the insurgents taking all the horses belonging to the government at Monterey, setting the governor and all his troops on foot. He raised a few horses as best he could and pursued them, but could not overtake them on foot. However, I understood that a sort of parley took place at or near San José, but no battle, surrender, or

OLD SPANISH BARRACKS AT MONTEREY.

settlement. Meanwhile, having started to return by land to Sutter's Fort, two hundred miles distant, I met the governor returning to Monterey. He stopped his forces and talked with me half an hour and confided to me his plans. He desired me to beg the Americans to be loyal to Mexico; to assure them that he was their friend, and in due time would give them all the lands to which they were entitled. He sent particularly friendly word to Sutter. Then I went on to the Mission of San José and there fell in with the insurgents, who had made that place their headquarters; I staid all night, and the leaders, Castro and Alvarado, treated me like a prince. The two insurgents protested their friendship for the Americans, and sent a request to Sutter to support them. On my arrival at the fort the situation was fully considered, and all, with a single exception, concluded to support Micheltorena. He had been our friend; he had granted us land; he promised, and we felt that we could rely upon, his continued friendship; and we felt, indeed we knew, we could not repose the same confi-

46

dence in the native Californians. This man Pablo Gutierrez, who had told me about the gold in the Sierra Nevada, was a native of Sinaloa in Mexico, and sympathized with the Mexican governor and with us. Sutter sent him with despatches to the governor, stating that we were organizing and preparing to join him. Pablo returned, and was sent again to tell the governor that we were on the march to join him at Monterey. This time he was taken prisoner with our despatches and was hanged to a tree, somewhere near the present town of Gilroy. That of course put an end to our gold discovery; otherwise Pablo Gutierrez might have been the discoverer instead of Marshall.[1]

But I still had it in my mind to try to find gold; so early in the spring of 1845 I made it a point to visit the mines in the south discovered by Ruelle in 1841. They were in the mountains about twenty miles north or northeast of the Mission of San Fernando, or say fifty miles from Los Angeles. I wanted to see the Mexicans working there, and to gain what knowledge I could of gold digging. Dr. John Townsend went with me. Pablo's confidence that there was gold on Bear River was fresh in my mind; and I hoped the same year to find time to return there and explore, and if possible find gold in the Sierra Nevada. But I had no time that busy year to carry out my purpose. The Mexicans' slow and inefficient manner of working the mine was most discouraging.

---

[1] The insurrection ended in the capitulation—I might call it expulsion—of Micheltorena. The causes which led to this result were various, some of them infamous. Pio Pico, being the oldest member of the Departmental Assembly, became governor, and Castro commander-in-chief of the military. They reigned but one year, and then came the Mexican war. Castro was made governor of Lower California, and died there. Pio Pico was not a vindictive man; he was a mild governor.

Pio Pico   James W. Marshall

When I returned to Sutter's Fort the same spring Sutter desired
me to engage with him for a year as bookkeeper, which meant his
general business man as well. His financial matters being in a bad
way, I consented. I had a great deal to do besides keeping the
books. Among other undertakings we sent men southeast in the
Sierra Nevada about forty miles from the fort to saw lumber with
a whipsaw. Two men would saw of good timber about one hundred or one hundred and twenty-five feet a day. Early in July I
framed an excuse to go into the mountains to give the men some
special directions about lumber needed at the fort. The day was
one of the hottest I had ever experienced. No place looked favorable for a gold discovery. I even attempted to descend into a
deep gorge through which meandered a small stream, but gave

it up on account of the brush and the heat. My search was fruit-less. The place where Marshall discovered gold in 1848 was about forty miles to the north of the saw-pits at this place. The next spring, 1849, I joined a party to go to the mines on and south of the Cosumne and Mokelumne rivers. The first day we reached a trading post—Digg's, I think, was the name. Several traders had there pitched their tents to sell goods. One of them was Tom Fallon, whom I knew. This post was within a few miles of where Sutter's men sawed the lumber in 1845. I asked Fallon if he had ever seen the old saw-pits where Sicard and Dupas had worked in 1845. He said he had, and knew the place well. Then I told him how I had attempted that year to descend into the deep gorge to the south of it to look for gold.

"My stars!" he said. "Why, that gulch down there was one of the richest placers that have ever been found in this country"; and he told me of men who had taken out a pint cupful of nuggets before breakfast.

Frémont's first visit to California was in the month of March, 1844. He came *via* eastern Oregon, traveling south and passing east of the Sierra Nevada, and crossed the chain about opposite the bay of San Francisco, at the head of the American River, and descended into the Sacramento Valley to Sutter's Fort. It was there I first met him. He staid but a short time, three or four weeks perhaps, to refit with fresh mules and horses and such provisions as he could obtain, and then set out on his return to the United States. Coloma, where Marshall afterward discovered gold, was on one of the branches of the American River. Frémont probably came down that very stream. How strange that he and his scientific corps did not discover signs of gold, as Commodore

Wilkes's party had done when coming overland from Oregon in 1841! One morning at the breakfast table at Sutter's, Frémont was urged to remain a while and go to the coast, and among other things which it would be of interest for him to see was mentioned a very large redwood tree *(Sequoia sempervirens)* near Santa Cruz, or rather a cluster of trees, forming apparently a single trunk, which was said to be seventy-two feet in circumference. I then told Frémont of the big tree I had seen in the Sierra Nevada in October, 1841, which I afterwards verified to be one of the fallen big trees of the Calaveras Grove. I therefore believe myself to have been the first white man to see the mammoth trees of California. The Sequoias are found nowhere except in California. The redwood that I speak of is the *Sequoia sempervirens,* and is confined to the sea-coast and the west side of the Coast Range Mountains. The *Sequoia gigantea,* or mammoth tree, is found only on the western slope of the Sierra Nevada—nowhere farther north than latitude 38° 30'.

Sutter's Fort was an important point from the very beginning of the colony. The building of the fort and all subsequent immigrations added to its importance, for that was the first point of destination to those who came by way of Oregon or direct across the plains. The fort was begun in 1842 and finished in 1844. There was no town till after the gold discovery in 1848, when it became the bustling, buzzing center for merchants, traders, miners, etc., and every available room was in demand. In 1849 Sacramento City was laid off on the river two miles west of the fort, and the town grew up there at once into a city. The first town was laid off by Hastings and myself in the month of January, 1846, about three or four miles below the mouth of the

American River, and called Sutterville. But first the Mexican war, then the lull which always follows excitement, and then the rush and roar of the gold discovery, prevented its building up till it was too late. Attempts were several times made to revive Sutterville, but Sacramento City had become too strong to be removed. Sutter always called his colony and fort "New Helvetia," in spite of which the name mostly used by others, before the Mexican war, was Sutter's Fort, or Sacramento, and later Sacramento altogether.

Sutter's many enterprises continued to create a growing demand for lumber. Every year, and sometimes more than once, he sent parties into the mountains to explore for an available site to build a sawmill on the Sacramento River or some of its tributaries, by which the lumber could be rafted down to the fort. There was no want of timber or of water power in the mountains, but the cañon features of the streams rendered rafting impracticable. The year after the war (1847) Sutter's needs for lumber were even greater than ever, although his embarrassments had increased and his ability to undertake new enterprises became less and less. Yet, never discouraged, nothing daunted, another hunt must be made for a sawmill site. This time Marshall happened to be the man chosen by Sutter to search the mountains. He was gone about a month, and returned with a most favorable report.

James W. Marshall went across the plains to Oregon in 1844, and thence came to California the next year. He was a wheelwright by trade, but, being very ingenious, he could turn his hand to almost anything. So he acted as carpenter for Sutter, and did many other things, among which I may mention making

ON THE SACRAMENTO RIVER.

wheels for spinning wool, and looms, reeds, and shuttles for weaving yarn into coarse blankets for the Indians, who did the carding, spinning, weaving, and all other labor. In 1846 Marshall went through the war to its close as a private. Besides his ingenuity as a mechanic, he had most singular traits. Almost every one pronounced him half crazy or hare-brained. He was certainly eccentric, and perhaps somewhat flighty. His insanity, however, if he had any, was of a harmless kind; he was neither vicious nor quarrelsome. He had great, almost overweening, confidence in his ability to do anything as a mechanic. I wrote the contract between Sutter and him to build the mill. Sutter was to furnish the means; Marshall was to build and run the mill, and have a share of the lumber for his compensation. His idea was to haul the lumber part way and raft it down the American River to Sacramento, and thence, his part of it, down the Sacramento River, and through Suisun and San Pablo bays to San Francisco for a market. Marshall's mind, in some respects at least, must have been unbalanced. It is hard to conceive how any sane man could have been so wide of the mark, or how any one could have selected such a site for a sawmill under the circumstances. Surely no other man than Marshall ever entertained so wild a scheme as that of rafting sawed lumber down the cañons of the American River, and no other man than Sutter would have been so confiding and credulous as to patronize him. It is proper to say that, under great difficulties, enhanced by winter rains, Marshall succeeded in building the mill — a very good one, too, of the kind.

SUTTER'S MILL.

It had improvements which I had never seen in sawmills, and I had had considerable experience in Ohio. But the mill would not run because the wheel was placed too low. It was an old-fashioned flutter wheel that propelled an upright saw. The gravelly bar below the mill backed the water up, and submerged and stopped the wheel. The remedy was to dig a channel or tail-race through the bar below to conduct away the water. The wild Indians of the mountains were employed to do the digging. Once through the bar there would be plenty of fall. The digging was hard and took some weeks. As soon as the water began to run through the tail-race the wheel was blocked, the gate raised, and the water permitted to gush through all night. It was Marshall's custom to examine the race while the water was running through in the morning, so as to direct the Indians where to deepen it, and then shut off the water for them to work during the day. The water was clear as crystal, and the current was swift enough to sweep away the sand and lighter materials. Marshall made these examinations early in the morning while the Indians were getting their breakfast. It was on one of these occasions, in the clear shallow water, that he saw something bright and yellow. He picked it up — it was a piece of gold! The world has seen and felt the result. The mill sawed little or no lumber; as a lumber enterprise the project was a failure, but as a gold discovery it was a grand success.

There was no excitement at first, nor for three or four months —because the mine was not known to be rich, or to exist anywhere except at the sawmill, or to be available to any one except Sutter, to whom every one conceded that it belonged. Time does not permit me to relate how I carried the news of the discovery to San Francisco; how the same year I discovered gold on Feather River and worked it; how I made the first weights and scales to weigh the first gold for Sam Brannan; how the richness of the mines became known by the Mormons who were employed by Sutter to work at the sawmill, working about on Sundays and finding it in the crevices along the stream and taking it to Brannan's store at the fort, and how Brannan kept the gold a secret as long as he could till the excitement burst out all at once like wildfire.

Among the notable arrivals at Sutter's Fort should be mentioned that of Castro and Castillero, in the fall of 1845. The latter had been before in California, sent, as he had been this time, as a peace commissioner from Mexico. Castro was so jealous that it was almost impossible for Sutter to have anything like a private interview with him. Sutter, however, was given to understand that, as he had stood friendly to Governor Micheltorena on the side of Mexico in the late troubles, he might rely on the friendship of Mexico, to which he was enjoined to continue faithful in all emergencies. Within a week Castillero was shown at San José a singular heavy reddish rock, which had long been known to the Indians, who rubbed it on their hands and faces to paint them. The Californians had often tried to smelt this rock in a blacksmith's fire, thinking it to be silver or some other precious metal. But Castillero, who was an intelligent man and a native of Spain, at once recognized it as quicksilver, and noted its resemblance to the cinnabar in the mines of Almaden. A company was immediately formed to work it, of which Castillero, Castro, Alexander Forbes, and others were members. The discovery of quicksilver at this time seems providential in view of its absolute necessity to supplement the imminent discovery of gold, which stirred and waked into new life the industries of the world.

It is a question whether the United States could have stood the shock of the great rebellion of 1861 had the California gold discovery not been made. Bankers and business men of New York in 1864 did not hesitate to admit that but for the gold of California, which monthly poured its five or six millions into that financial center, the bottom would have dropped out of everything. These timely arrivals so strengthened the nerves of trade and stimulated business as to enable the Government to sell its bonds at a time when its credit was its lifeblood and the main reliance by which to feed, clothe, and maintain its armies. Once our bonds went down to thirty-eight cents on the dollar. California gold averted a total collapse, and enabled a preserved Union to come forth from the great conflict with only four billions of debt instead of a hundred billions. The hand of Providence so plainly seen in the discovery of gold is no less manifest in the time chosen for its accomplishment.

PART TWO

IN THE AUTUMN of 1845 Frémont came on his second exploring expedition to California. This time he divided his party east of the Sierra Nevada and sent the greater portion to come in through a gap supposed to exist farther to the south, while he followed substantially what is now the emigrant road, or Truckee route, and came direct to Sutter's Fort with about eight or nine men. At that time I was in charge of Sutter's Fort and of Sutter's business, he being absent at the bay of San Francisco. Frémont camped on the American River about three miles above the fort. The first notice of his return to California was his sudden appearance, with Kit Carson, at the fort. He at once made known to me his wants, namely, sixteen mules, six pack-saddles, some flour and other provisions, and the use of a blackmith's shop to shoe the mules, to enable him to go in haste to meet the others of his party. I told him precisely what could and could not be furnished —that we had no mules, but could let him have horses, and could make the pack-saddles; that he might have the use of a black-smith's shop, but we were entirely out of coal. He became reticent, and, saying something in a low tone to Kit Carson, rose and left without saying good-day, and returned to his camp. As they mounted their horses to leave, Frémont was heard to say that I was unwilling to accommodate him, which greatly pained me;

for, of course, we were always glad of the arrival of Americans, and especially of one in authority. Besides, I knew that Captain Sutter would do anything in his power for Frémont. So I took with me Dr. Gildea, a recent arrival from St. Louis, across the plains, and hastened to Frémont's camp and told him what had been reported to me. He stated, in a very formal manner, that he was the officer of one government and Sutter the officer of another; that difficulties existed between those governments; and hence his inference that I, representing Sutter, was not willing to accommodate him. He reminded me that on his first arrival here, in 1844, Sutter had sent out and in half an hour had brought

SAN FRANCISCO.

him all the mules he wanted. I protested my willingness to do anything in my power, but was obliged to plead inability to do more than stated, telling him that in 1844 Sutter was in far better circumstances; that on that occasion a man (Peter Lassen) had just arrived with a hundred mules, of which Sutter had bought what Frémont needed. But he had not been able to pay for them, because Frémont's drafts had to go East before Sutter could realize on them the money which had been promised to Lassen. In a few days Sutter returned, but could not furnish anything more than I had offered. Then Frémont concluded to go down to the bay and get supplies. He went with his little party of eight or nine men, including Kit Carson, but without success; so he sent the men back to Sutter's Fort to go, as best they could, to find the main party. Meanwhile he himself had made his way to Monterey to see the American consul, Thomas O. Larkin. After several weeks Frémont and his entire party became united in the San Joaquin Valley.[1] While at Monterey he had obtained permission from José Castro, the commandant-general, to winter in the San Joaquin Valley, away from the settlements, where the men

---

[1] His men in the mountains had suffered considerably. Frémont had given positive orders for them to wait at a certain gap or low divide till he should meet them with supplies, but the place could not be found. The men got out of provisions and bought from the Indians. The kind they most relished was a sort of brown meal, which was rich and spicy, and came so much into favor that they wanted no other. After a while the Indians became careless in the preparation of this wonderful meal, when it was discovered to be full of the broken wings and legs of grasshoppers! It was simply dried grasshoppers pounded into a meal. The men said it was rich and would stick to the mouth like gingerbread, and that they were becoming sleek and fat. But after the discovery they lost their appetites. How hard it is sometimes to overcome prejudice!

would not be likely to annoy the people. He had in all in the exploring party about sixty well-armed men. He also had permission to extend his explorations in the spring as far south as the Colorado River.

Accordingly early in the spring (1846) Frémont started south with his party. When Castro gave him permission to explore towards the Colorado River he no doubt supposed he would go south or southeast from where he was camped in the San Joaquin Valley, and on through the Tejon Pass and the Mojave Desert; but, instead, Frémont with his sixty armed men started to go west and southwest through the most thickly settled parts of California, namely, the Santa Clara, Pajaro, and Salinas valleys. As he was approaching the last valley Castro sent an official order by an officer warning Frémont that he must leave, as his action was illegal. The order was delivered March 5. Frémont took possession of an eminence called Gavilan Peak, and continued to fortify himself for several days, perhaps a week or more, Castro meantime remaining in sight and evidently increasing his force day by day. Frémont, enraged against Castro, finally abandoned his position in the night of March 9, and, gaining the San Joaquin Valley, made his way rapidly northward up the Sacramento Valley and into Oregon, leaving Sutter's about March 24.

A little over four weeks after Frémont left I happened to be fishing four or five miles down the Sacramento River, having then left Sutter's service with the view of trying to put up two or three hundred barrels of salmon, thinking the venture would be profitable. An officer of the United States, Lieutenant A. H. Gillespie, of the marines, bearing messages to the explorer, came up the river in a small boat and at once inquired about Frémont.

JOHN C. FREMONT.

I told him he had gone to Oregon. Said he: "I want to overhaul him. How far is it to the fort?" And receiving my reply, he pushed rapidly on. He overtook Frémont near the Oregon line. Frémont, still indignant against Castro, who had compelled him to abandon his explorations south, returned at once to California. It so happened that Castro had sent Lieutenant Arce to the north side of the bay of San Francisco to collect scattered Government horses. Arce had secured about one hundred and fifty and was taking them to the south side of the bay, *via* Sutter's Fort and the San Joaquin Valley. This was the only way to transfer cattle or horses from one side of the bay to the other, except at the Straits of Carquinez by the slow processes of swimming one at a time, or of taking one or two, tied by all four feet, in a small boat or launch. Arce, with the horses and seven or eight soldiers, arrived at Sutter's Fort, staid overnight as the guest of Sutter, and went on his way to the Cosumne River (about sixteen or eighteen miles) and camped for the night.

Frémont's hasty departure for Oregon and Gillespie's pursuit of him had been the occasion of many surmises. Frémont's sud-

THOMAS O. LARKIN   MARIANO G. VALLEJO

KIT CARSON   JOHN BIDWELL

den return excited increased curiosity. People flocked to his camp: some were settlers, some hunters; some were good men, and some about as rough specimens of humanity as it would be possible to find anywhere. Frémont, hearing that the horses were passing, sent a party of these promiscuous people and captured them. This of course was done before he had orders or any positive news that war had been declared. When Gillespie left the United States, as the bearer of a despatch to Larkin and Frémont and of letters to the latter, war had not been declared. The letters included one from Senator Benton, who had the confidence and knew the purposes of the Administration. As Gillespie had to make his way through Mexico, he committed the despatch and his orders to memory, destroyed them, and rewrote them on the vessel which took him, *via* the Sandwich Islands, to the coast of

California. There had been no later arrival, and therefore no later despatches to Frémont were possible. Though Frémont was reticent, whatever he did was supposed to be done with the sanction of the United States. Thus, without giving the least notice even to Sutter, the great friend of Americans, or to Americans in general, scattered and exposed as they were all over California, he precipitated the war.

Sutter was always outspoken in his wish that some day California should belong to the United States; but when he heard that the horses had been taken from Arce (who made no resistance, but with his men and with insulting messages was permitted to go on his way to Castro at Santa Clara), he expressed surprise that Captain Frémont had committed such an act without his knowledge. What Sutter had said was reported to Frémont, perhaps with some exaggeration.

As soon as the horses arrived at Frémont's camp, the same party—about twenty-five in number—were sent to Sonoma. By this party General Vallejo, the most prominent Californian north of the bay, his brother Salvador, his brother-in-law Jacob P. Leese, and Victor Prudon were surprised at night, taken prisoners, and conveyed to Frémont's camp, over eighty miles distant by the traveled route on the Sacramento River. The prisoners were sent to Sutter's Fort, Frémont arriving at the same time. Then Sutter and Frémont met, face to face, for the first time since Frémont, a month before, had passed on his way towards Oregon. I do not know what words passed between them; I was near, but did not hear. This, however, I know, that Sutter had become elated, as all Americans were, with the idea that what Frémont was doing meant California for the United States. But in a few

VALLEJO'S ADOBE HOME AT SONOMA.

minutes Sutter came to me greatly agitated, with tears in his eyes, and said that Frémont had told him he was a Mexican, and that if he did not like what he (Frémont) was doing he would set him across the San Joaquin River and he could go and join the Mexicans. But, this flurry over, Sutter was soon himself again, and resumed his normal attitude of friendship towards Frémont, because he thought him to be acting in accordance with instructions from Washington. For want of a suitable prison, the prisoners were placed in Sutter's parlor,—a large room in the southwest corner of the second story of the two-story adobe house,—which had but one door, and this was now guarded by a sentinel. Frémont gave me special directions about the safety of the prisoners, and I understood him to put them under my special charge. Some of Frémont's men remained at the fort.

Among the men who remained to hold Sonoma was William

B. Ide, who assumed to be in command. In some way (perhaps through an unsatisfactory interview with Frémont which he had before the move on Sonoma) Ide got the notion that Frémont's hand in these events was uncertain, and that Americans ought to strike for an independent republic. To this end nearly every day he wrote something in the form of a proclamation and posted it on the old Mexican flagstaff. Another man left at Sonoma was William L. Todd,[1] who painted, on a piece of brown cotton, a yard and a half or so in length, with old red or brown paint that he happened to find, what he intended to be a representation of a grizzly bear. This was raised to the top of the staff, some seventy feet from the ground. Native Californians looking up at it were heard to say *"Coche,"* the common name among them for pig or shoat.

The party at Sonoma now received some accessions from Americans and other foreigners living on the north side of the bay. Rumors began to reach them of an uprising on the part of the native Californians, which indeed began under Joaquin de la Torre. Henry L. Ford and other Americans to the number of thirty met De la Torre — whose force was said to number from forty to eighty — near the Petaluma Ranch, and four or five of the Californians were said to have been killed or wounded. The repulse of the Californians seems to have been complete, though reports continued alarming, and a man sent from Sonoma to

_____

[1] More than thirty years afterwards I chanced to meet Todd on the train coming up the Sacramento Valley. He had not greatly changed, but appeared considerably broken in health. He informed me that Mrs. Lincoln was his own aunt, and that he had been brought up in the family of Abraham Lincoln.

THE ORIGINAL BEAR FLAG.

Russian River for powder was killed. A messenger was sent in haste to Sacramento for Frémont, who hurried to Sonoma with nearly all his exploring party and scoured the country far and near, but found no enemy.

I tried to make the prisoners at Sacramento as comfortable as possible, assisting to see that their meals were regularly and properly brought, and sometimes I would sit by while they were eating. One day E. M. Kern, artist to Frémont's exploring expedition, called me out and said it was Frémont's orders that no one was to go in or speak to the prisoners. I told him they were in my charge, and that he had nothing to say about them. He asserted that they were in his charge, and finally convinced me that he had been made an equal, if not the principal, custodian. I then told him that, as both of us were not needed, I would go over and join Frémont at Sonoma. Just at this time Lieutenant

Washington A. Bartlett of the United States Navy arrived from the bay, inquiring for Frémont. The taking of the horses from Arce, the capture of the prisoners, and the occupation of Sonoma, had been heard of, and he was sent to learn what it meant. So he went over to Sonoma with me.

On our arrival Frémont was still absent trying to find the enemy, but that evening he returned. The Bear Flag was still flying, and had been for a week or more. The American flag was nowhere displayed. There was much doubt about the situation. Frémont gave us to understand that we must organize. Lieutenant Gillespie seemed to be his confidential adviser and spokesman, and said that a meeting would be held the next day at which Frémont would make an address. He also said that it would be necessary to have some plan of organization ready to report to the meeting; and that P. B. Reading, W. B. Ide, and myself were requested to act as a committee to report such a plan. We could learn nothing from Frémont or Gillespie to the effect that the United States had anything to do with Frémont's present movements.

In past years, rumors of threats against Americans in California had been rather frequent, several times causing them and other foreigners to hasten in the night from all places within one or two hundred miles to Sutter's Fort, sometimes remaining a week or two, drilling and preparing to resist attack. The first scare of this kind occurred in 1841, when Sutter became somewhat alarmed; the last, in 1845. But in every case such rumors had proved to be groundless, so that Americans had ceased to have apprehensions, especially in the presence of such an accessible refuge as Sutter's Fort. And now, in 1846, after so many accessions by immigration, we felt entirely secure, even without the presence of a United States officer and his exploring force of sixty men, until we found ourselves suddenly plunged into a war. But hostilities having been begun, bringing danger where none before existed, it now became imperative to organize. It was in every one's mouth (and I think must have come from Frémont) that the war was begun in defense of American settlers! This was simply a pretense to justify the premature beginning of the war, which henceforth was to be carried on in the name of the United States.

So much has been said and written about the "Bear Flag" that some may conclude it was something of importance. It was not so regarded at the time: it was never adopted at any meeting or by any agreement; it was, I think, never even noticed, perhaps never seen, by Frémont when it was flying. The naked old Mexican flagstaff at Sonoma suggested that something should be put on it. Todd had painted it, and others had helped to put it up, for mere pastime. It had no importance to begin with, none whatever when the Stars and Stripes went up, and never would have been thought of again had not an officer of the navy seen it in Sonoma and written a letter about it.

Under these circumstances on the Fourth of July our committee met. We soon found that we could not agree. Ide wished to paste together his long proclamations on the flagstaff, and make them our report. Reading wrote something much shorter, which I thought still too long. I proposed for our report simply this: "The undersigned hereby agree to organize for the purpose of gaining and maintaining the independence of California." Unable to agree upon a report, we decided to submit what we had written to Lieutenant Gillespie, without our names, and ask him to choose. He chose mine. The meeting took place, but Frémont's remarks gave us no light upon any phase of the situation. He neither averred nor denied that he was acting under orders from the United States Government. Some men had been guilty of misconduct in an Indian village, and he reprimanded them — said he wanted nothing to do with the movement unless the men would conduct themselves properly. Gillespie made some remarks, presented the report, and all present signed it.

The organization took place forthwith, by the formation of three companies. The captains elected were Henry L. Ford, Granville P. Swift, and Samuel J. Hensley. Thus organized, we marched into the Sacramento Valley. The men who had not been at Sonoma signed the report at the camp above Sutter's Fort, except a few who soon after signed it at the Mokelumne River on our march to Monterey. This was, so far as I know, the last seen or heard of that document, for Commodore Sloat had raised the American flag at Monterey before our arrival, and soon it waved in all places in California where American influence prevailed.

As yet, Frémont had received advices from Washington no later than those brought by Gillespie. His object in going to Monterey must have been to confer with Commodore Sloat and get positive information about the war with Mexico, which proved to be a reality, as we learned even before our arrival there. There

"The undersigned hereby agree to organize for the purpose of gaining and maintaining the independence of California".

THE BEAR FLAG PLATFORM (BIDWELL'S HANDWRITING).

was now no longer uncertainty; all were glad. It was a glorious sight to see the Stars and Stripes as we marched into Monterey. Here we found Commodore Sloat. The same evening, or the next, Commodore Stockton, a chivalrous and dashing officer, arrived around Cape Horn to supersede him. Plans were immediately laid to conquer California. A California Battalion was to be organized, and Frémont was to be lieutenant-colonel in command. Stockton asked Frémont to nominate his own officers. P. B. Reading was chosen paymaster, Ezekiel Merritt quartermaster, and, I think, King, commissary. The captains and lieutenants chosen at Sonoma were also commissioned. Though I did not aspire to office, I received a commission as second lieutenant.

Merritt, the quartermaster, could neither read nor write. He was an old mountaineer and trapper, lived with an Indian squaw, and went clad in buckskin fringed after the style of the Rocky Mountain Indians. He chewed tobacco to a disgusting excess, and stammered badly. He had a reputation for bravery because of his continual boasting of his prowess in killing Indians. The handle of the tomahawk he carried had nearly a hundred notches to record the number of his Indian scalps. He drank deeply whenever he could get liquor. Stockton said to him: "Major Merritt" (for he was now major), "make out a requisition for some money, say two thousand dollars. You will need about that amount at the start. Bring your requisition on board, and I will approve, and direct the purser to honor it." Major Reading wrote the requisition and Merritt got the money, two thousand Mexican silver dollars. That afternoon I met him in Monterey, nearly as drunk as he could be. He said, "Bidwell, I am rich; I have lots of money"; and putting both hands into the deep pockets of his buckskin breeches he brought out two handfuls of Mexican dollars, saying, "Here, take this, and if you can find anything to buy, buy it, and when you want more money come to me, for I have got lots of it."

Merritt was never removed from his office or rank, but simply fell into disuse, and was detailed, like subordinate officers or men, to perform other duties, generally at the head of small scouting parties. Merritt's friends—for he must have had friends to recommend him for quartermaster—in some way managed to fix up the accounts relating to the early administration of his office. In fact, I tried to help them myself, but I believe that all of us together were never able to find, within a thousand dollars, what Merritt had done with the money. How he ever came to be recommended for quartermaster was to every one a mystery. Perhaps some of the current theories that subsequently prevailed might have had in them just a shade of truth, namely, that somebody entertained the idea that quartermaster meant the ability and duty to quarter the beef!

The first conquest of California, in 1846, by the Americans, with the exception of the skirmish at Petaluma and another towards Monterey, was achieved without a battle. We simply marched all over California from Sonoma to San Diego and raised the American flag without opposition or protest. We tried to find an enemy, but could not. So Kit Carson and Ned Beale were sent East, bearing despatches from Commodore Stockton announcing the entire conquest of California by the United States. Frémont was made governor by Stockton at Los Angeles, but could not enter upon the full discharge of the duties of his office till he had visited the upper part of California and returned.

Commodore Robert F. Stockton.

He sent me to take charge of the Mission of San Luis Rey, with a commission as magistrate over the larger portion of the country between Los Angeles and San Diego. Stockton and all his forces retired on board of their vessels. Frémont went north, leaving part of his men at Los Angeles under Gillespie, part at Santa Barbara under Lieutenant Talbot, and some at other points. Pio Pico and José Castro, respectively the last Mexican governor and commander-in-chief, remained concealed a while and then withdrew into Mexico.

Suddenly, in about a month, Frémont being in the north and his troops scattered, the whole country south of Monterey was in a state of revolt. Then for the first time there was something like war. As there were rumors of Mexican troops coming from Sonora, Merritt was sent by Gillespie to reconnoiter towards the Colorado River. Gillespie was surrounded at Los Angeles, and made to capitulate. I fled from San Luis Rey to San Diego. Merritt and his party, hearing of the outbreak, also escaped to San Diego. Meanwhile Frémont enlisted a considerable force (about four hundred), principally from the large Hastings immigration at Sacramento, and marched south. Commodore Stockton had landed and marched to retake Los Angeles, and failed. All the men-of-war, and all the scattered forces, except Frémont's new force, were then concentrated at San Diego, where Commodore Stockton collected and reorganized the forces, composed of sailors, marines, men of Frémont's battalion under Gillespie and Merritt, volunteers at San Diego, including some native Californians and that portion of the regular troops under General S. W. Kearney that had escaped from the field of San Pascual — in all between 700 and 800 men. Of these forces I was commissioned

GENERAL STEPHEN W. KEARNY.

and served as quartermaster. This work of preparation took several months. Finally, on the 29th of December, 1846, the army set out to retake Los Angeles. It fought the battles of San Gabriel and the Mesa, which ended the insurrection. The enemy fled, met Frémont at San Fernando, and surrendered to him the next day. The terms of surrender were so lenient that the native Californians from that time forth became the fast friends of Frémont.

Unfortunate differences regarding rank had arisen between Stockton and Kearney. Frémont was afterwards arrested in California by Kearney for refusing to obey his orders, and was taken to Washington and court-martialed. Stockton, however, was largely to blame. He would not submit to General Kearney, his superior in command on land, and that led Frémont to refuse to obey Kearney, his superior officer. Frémont's disobedience was no doubt owing to the advice of Stockton, who had appointed him governor of California.[1]

The war being over, nearly all the volunteers were discharged from the service in February and March, 1847, at Los Angeles and San Diego. Most of us made our way up the coast by land to our homes. I had eleven horses, which I swam, one at a time, across the Straits of Carquinez at Benicia, which J. M. Hudspeth, the surveyor, was at the time laying out for Dr. Robert Semple, and which was then called "Francisca," after Mrs. Vallejo, whose maiden name was Francisca Benicia Carrillo.

---

[1] It was reported in 1890 that General Vallejo in one of his letters tells of having received on the same day communications from Commodore Stockton, General Kearney, and Colonel Frémont, each one signing himself "Commander-in-chief of California."

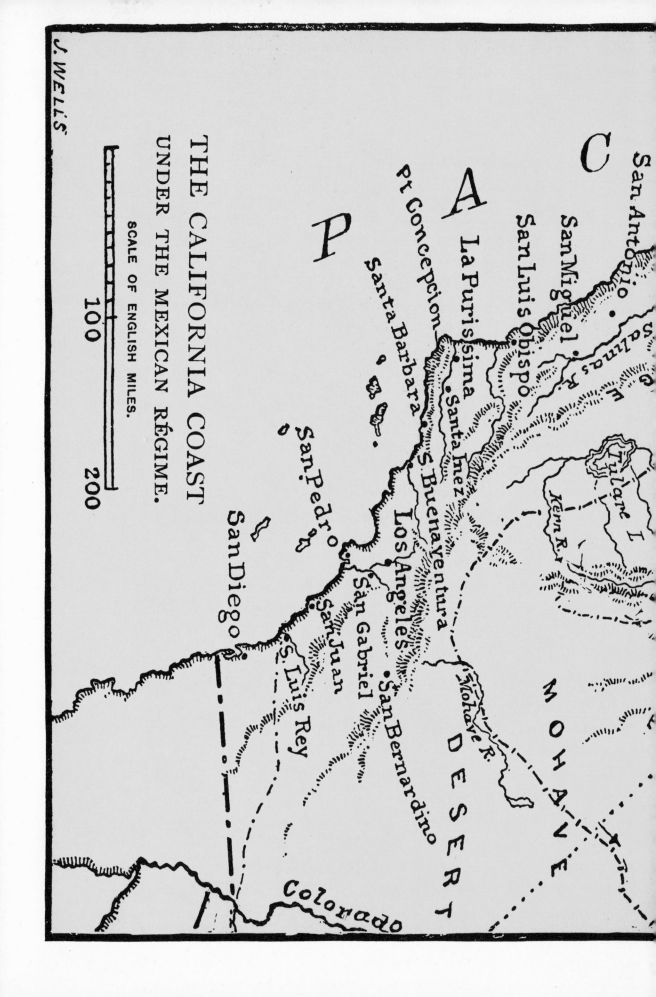

THE CALIFORNIA COAST
UNDER THE MEXICAN RÉGIME.

SCALE OF ENGLISH MILES.

100   200

J. WELLS.

C

San Antonio.

San Miguel.

A   San Luis Obispo

La Purissima

Pt Concepcion

P   Santa Inez

Santa Barbara

S. Buenaventura

San Pedro

Los Angeles

San Gabriel

San Juan

S. Luis Rey

San Diego

San Bernardino

Salinas R.

Tulare I.

Kern R.

Mohave R.

MOHAVE

DESERT

Colorado